Anaahata

Anaahata

Sandhya S. Nayar

Calligraphy
Siddharth Adésara

PARTRIDGE

A Penguin Random House Company

To order additional copies of this book, contact
Partridge India
000 800 10062 62
orders.india@partridgepublishing.com

www.partridgepublishing.com/india

An offering
At the altar of
Satyam Shivam Sundaram
Truth Virtue Beauty
Manifested
In all their pristine glory
In my Divine Master
Sri Sri Paramahansa Yogananda

Dedicated to
My Heavenly Father
and His perfect embodiment
My earthly father
Prof.T.K.S. Nayar

1

Thou impregnated me
In ruby hued Muladhara
With Ganesha
Sculpted from Mother's being
Loyal Doorkeeper
Fiery protector
Father's long illumined shadow
Remover of debris
That clog the royal path
My Son in seed
Love nurtured
Grace cocooned
Promise honoured
Time crowned

2

The ether holds secrets
Of all thoughts ever thought
All feelings ever felt
All lives ever lived
To be caught and chronicled
For the ghosts to rest in peace

3

As creation flows
I add or erase
A word here
A verse there
In the midst
Of every breath
Is this how Master Sculptor
Thou chisel and smooth
The finest vein
Or the grandest cloak
On my soul rock?

4

As my loved one
Almost slipped away
Like a precious dew
From a lotus leaf
Thy swift gentle hands
Recalled it back
A stilled shining diamond
On Thy little finger
And Thy clear voice whispered
A sage counsel
All this a fleeting validation
Of being calmly active
The ripened fruit
Of being actively calm

5

What hope or plan
Applause or disdain
When all we need
Is to rush into
Thy palatial heart
All a smoke dream
In a beautiful mist

6

Birds of prey
Peck mercilessly
An injured brethren
Unafraid of Thy thunderbolt
Hidden among the clouds

7

Time fills in
Footprints in sand
But gnaws afresh
Filled wounds
On bloodmarked days
Like the wails of an infant
Jerks awake
The exhausted mother
From midnight's silent womb

8

Suffering
The sharp thrust
Of the gold stem
That cradles the joy jewel
The lone journey
Through the wombal slush
Of the treasured infant
Welcomed by brimming bosom

9

Flesh struggles
To clasp spirit
In loving familiarity
Thy torrential forces
Threaten to uproot
In a cruel giant sweep
Like a ripened fruit
Hidden in the green
Escapes the eagle eye
But not the multifarious claws
Of the antal regiment

10

I brought a thimble
To the ocean
And got a drop
That vaporised
In the sweltering sun
Then a cupful
Which spilled
As I stumbled along
Later a barrel
But the graced brine
Leaked unawares
And bloomed a garden
On the desert patch
Now weary and lost
I faced the ocean
With empty hands
That tore open
My blushing soul
And the ocean leaped
Into the treasure chest
Gurgling and rolling
In holy laughter

11

As a Master Sculptor
Thou art chiselling
The last bit
Of stubborn rock
The fine lines
That make or mar
A smile from a frown
The tear
That swims the eye
But too proud to brim
And overflow
To mingle salt with blood
In a pain clenched mouth

12

One dipped
In a volcano
Startles not
At stray fireworks

13

In the greenroom
Of quiet contemplation
I peel away
The mask
And the grease paint
Of accumulated incarnations
To watch from
The darkened gallery
The many roles and
Hollow bullets
The fireworks
And the funeral march
Of accomplished actors
On invisible strings
In the giant hands
Of the Master Director

14

Thou gave birth
In a bliss of laughter
Turning each peal
Into cosmic joybeats
We dive and search
Through every sense
The forgotten source
Of that pristine Laughter

15

My insides churned
And heaved
Like an ocean
In volcanic spate
With no release
In Earth's embrace
Or Heaven's suckle
All my gods are mocked
When the heart longs
For man's follies

16

In the circus
Of this chaotic world
All long to be ringmasters
None to clean
The filthy cage
All to ride atop the white steed
None to play the dwarfed clown

17

My will
A weak concubine
Shudders
At the thought of conquest
Like the warrior
Who throws words
Into the fire
In trust of the stars
Forgetting unsought clouds
Who shroud moon
Play dice with stars
And mock the designs
Of intricate constellations

18

I am the lightening
That whips
The naked back
Of the sky
The fragrance
Of the promised
First summer rain
I am the bird
That plunges
In a graceful hunt
And the fish
That bares its heart
To the feathered knife

19

At times a bleating sheep am I
Until in Thy heart lake
I see my lion mane
Often a restless ape
Swinging on innumerable desire boughs
Perhaps an elephant elegant
With calm conserved power
Or a dolphin divine
Playful in Thy oceanic expanse
Maybe a maverick cuckoo
Singing a hope song
To nudge awake the dawn
Perchance a thousand hooded serpent
Shielding quivering loved ones
But my soul longs
To be Thy supreme swan
Gliding gracefully
In Thine infinite mind lake

20

Suffering smelts
A nature noble
But lays waste
The base
As gold burnishes
Through fire
While coal
Crumbles to ash

21

Snake sheds skin
When the new
Is readied beneath
As Thou will
Burn this rag
When the intricately embellished
Wedding garment
Gets its final stitch

22

Nectared love
Possessively corked
Floats oblivious
In Thy Joy waters
Until stormy waves
Shatter fragile glass
For drop
To become ocean

23

For mere mortals
Strutting about
On loaned wealth
The audacity of prophets
Who mirror Thine inheritance
In their beggar's garb

24

Talent laments
For it's not enough
Genius suffers
For it's too much
But above sits
The Fool
Content and smiling

25

On the endless
Dark days of despair
I yearned
For the sunrise of Thy love
Knowing little
That the sun of Thy presence
Always shone bright
In the cleansed sky of my spirit
While the earth of my awareness
Rose and set
In Time's eternal play

26

Cleaning for Spring
I uprooted
Summer's mayhem
And Winter's feared clutter

27

Demand in joy
And the Heavens rain
An unseasonal harvest
Whimper a want
And often a lightening whiplash
Breaks your stooping back
The regal gates
Await
Heroic giants
The whining dwarfs
Lay crawling beneath

28

The Sun hides not
Her brilliance
In a shroud
Of shame
But lends
Her sister Night
An iridescent Moon
To tease
Clandestine lovers
Who under
Delusion's blanket
Sigh promises
Too lofty to fulfil

29

On a dark moonless night
The ocean in me
Dreamt itself a puddle
Wanton boys spat
And splashed
In their muddy feet
While treasures within
Wasted lay
In the caked salt
Until I heard
The mighty roar
Of Thy seven rivers
The puddle in me
Laughed itself
Into the Ocean again

30

A slow painful fear
Envelops my being
Anxiety trickles
Through every vein
Until fear and I
Lay down
Cheek to cheek
Lulled by
Thumping heartbeats

31

Thou hast drawn
A circle of fire
Around me
With the fiery finger
Of Thy will
I can't jump over it
Nor stay within
Its arid vapours
Only the cool showers
Of Thy grace
Can drench me
In invincibility

32

Divine Gardener
Thou ploughed
Pruned
Pickaxed
In my soul's
Winter
And now
Though outside
Autumn resides
Within Spring rejoices

33

Into my calm mind lake
Dive birds of prey
Tearing its silken solitude
While my oceanic being
In tranquil infinity
Receives leviathan boulders
From boisterous rivers
Like a falling feather
From a bird in flight

34

In life's chrysalis
The butterfly in me
Laughs at
That blob of flesh
So attached
To its wingless cage

35

When my gratitude cup
Spills over
Even a prayer
Of thankfulness
Is ingratitude
So wistful silence
Reigns

36

Let moments
Trickle in
What matters
Whether joy adorned
Or sorrow drenched?
Today confined
In a broken well
Tomorrow lashing
The saffroned horizon

37

Thou art aware
Of my infinitesimal
Thought beat
O the glory
And shame
Of it

38

I crawled away
From Thy cradle
As the hand
That was to rock it
Set it aflame
Now womb emptied
I long for
Thy bosom's comfort
Betrayed
Embittered
My heart stone
Cracks noiselessly
Bleeding milk

39

Thy Holy Grail
Waits
On the highest step
Of my Joy ladder
While my blinded self
Wails
As no coin clanks
In my beggar's
Dented tin mug

40

Time squandered
Is harvested anew
In eternity's seasons
But love indifferented
Burns in regrets
At the lengthening shadows
Of an incarnation's close

41

In Patience's harvest
Are delightful fruits
Seeds of which
Were never planted

42

This surrender
Is not of the
Wounded
Trembling
Vanquished
With hands entwined
Around the tyrant's feet
In mournful supplication
This surrender
Is a joyous anticipation
Of the infant
As the father
Throws him up
Against the wind
To catch
In a wondrous embrace

43

In pursuit of bliss
I laid to rest
The ill matched twins
Feeling brain
Thinking heart
And fed
Each love starved cell
Thy wondrous
Joytrons of peace

44

As I laugh
In quiet mirth
I marvel
How courage
And rebellion
Give birth
To unbridled moments
From human misery
That reckless song
Gut wrenched
To air stifled soul
Its moment
Of Edenic recollection

45

My obstinate
Faith grass
Cranes
Its crushed neck
Every morn
After twilight's
Hoofed trampling
And dawn's
Dewed tonic

46

I will despair not
When love
Heeds not Thy call
For when the oil
Is hot enough
The mustard seeds
Will splutter

47

As Thou shook
My soul awake
From incarnations of sleep
It lit around it
Perennial pain bonfires
The hard ignorance crust
Melts for it to breathe
The breathless breath
Long it reposed
In the seeming comfort
Of ceaseless pleasures
But castled in the thorns
Of poisonous fears

48

As little children
Mesmerized by marbles
Heed not the call
Of the Mother
You and I
Squabble over coins
As Death and Time
Keep watch

49

In the insipid slavery
Of masters
Flourish
The insolent mastery
Of slaves

50

On life's battlefield
A wounded warrior
Offers thee
His bleeding arm
As a crutch
To cover a distance
Not to cling
And be a creeper
Take root
Flower
Fruit
And turn help
To home

51

Thy grace bridge
Connects
My reason and feeling
While below roars
The sea of doubt

52

If many fathers
Does success have
Then failure
An orphan is
But an act spectacular
Is conceived always
Immaculately

53

Thou first wrote
The epilogue
And then rearranged
The play of scenes
To suit
The lofty end

54

I looked fear
In the eye
And the philander
Winked at me

55

Pain
Unexpected
Night guest
Assigned
Holiest room
In my Joy castle

56

What takes me
Lifetimes to untie
Is cut
In one stroke
By the other

57

In a pain ravaged face
I saw Thy spark
That had burnt
To cinders
My doll house

58

All the outlets
Have been sealed
The lake is filled
To the brim
Where else can it overflow
But to Thy valley?

59

Because I know
You will pass My Test
I test thee
Rejoice
And dip thy pen
In the love ink
For the night slate
Awaits thy lightening touch

60

To hate Good
Is to resist
God in self
But for how long?
Redemption awaits
Near the bend
In the road
But to despise Evil
Is to tempt
The lurking Devil
To build
Brick by brick
A tavern
In thy temple

61

Minds argue
Hearts judge
But Souls mingle
In an eternal
Homecoming

62

Thou pulled
The ego veil
From my puritan face
A divine promiscuity
Makes bold
My embracing eyes

63

My voracious heart
Denied in abstinence
Devours
In unembarrassed
Mouthfuls
All
At Thy love table

64

Even blossoms wild
Flower
Fruit
At Thy will
While I
Slumber
In mute resistance

65

Through the sorrows
Of another
I cry
But for my own

66

I will come
When all you need
Is Me
As success is
For him
With options none

67

Befriend Evil
And it swallows you
Into its vile void
But even an enmity
With Beauty
Liberates
As it annihilates

68

As I watch
Myself watch
The familiar
Becomes unknown
And the stranger
Is my own

69

Tons of tears
Wail for release
Move aside
Lunatic laughter
Reckless smiles
Deafening optimism
Let me gather
To my bosom
My long ignored tears
Lest the little ones
Wither and disappear
Leaving a heart moist
White and saline

70

When the whole creation is Thee
It little matters
Whether I play in Thy lap
Rock on Thy knees
Cling to Thy bosom
Or 'am tied to Thy back
Thy little one is content
And protected
Even in the shadow
Of Thy bejeweled toe

71

When all doors close
Thou blow off
The roof
To let in
Thy light

72

The scales of this life
Can never balanced be
For to the right
Is my Master
To the left
The world
A toxic heap
None can lift the other
An inch true
For to weigh my Master
Is to distil a rose
To imprison the fragrance
Of an eternal spring

73

As Thou walked
Pain ravaged desert lands
The hem of Thy holy robe
Entwined in a thorn
Thou stooped
And with gentle words
Of ceaseless sweetness
Worked Thy mercy fingers
To unthread thorn from fabric
But alas
The sharp spear pierced
Thy sacred flesh
A ruby drop slipped on thorn
Blood blossomed
A royal rose
Fragrant with grace
Blushing in bliss

74

I shall walk away
Not from love's lack
But from too much
As cloud rains not
On its own
But wind travels
For thirsty earth

75

My anger
A closed dish
Ferments
Spits
Into itself

76

I will not
Give up
Give in
Thy soldier am I
I merely follow orders
The plan is Thine
The war is Thine
But the victory is ours

77

Slowly the mist lifts
And I glimpse
Thy will
Like shooting stars
In a desert dark

78

My will I use
To attune to Thine
Then the pebble tiny
From the mountain top
Becomes a boulder giant
Crushing impediments all
On the journey swift
To the valley green

79

In my arid
Heart desert
Blows
Relentless dust storms
Exposing
Buried skeletons
Of caravans ravaged

80

In churning
Moments to hours
Wishes remain
Action naked
Like the sun
Turns ditch to rain
But the desert
Bakes in pain
Gentleness rises in surrender
While sand scorches
In stubborn aloofness

81

In the midst of strife
My soul wails
To cleave to Thee
In eternal forgetfulness

82

If pain preserves
Thy thought
Why made Thee joy?

83

When Thou decide
To reward
Reprimand
Reveal
We mere instruments
If reluctant
Thou pick up another
Intention done
But our chance missed
Thy glory lives on
In varied climes
Willing hands
Receptive hearts

84

The tree
Reflects the seed
As the sins
Of the father
Shadows the children
In a magical law
Of imitation

85

Who tells mind
To be aware
Come back
From wanderings?
Is it Thee?
Then it's Thee
Who controls
Illumines
Surpasses
Hiding
Under the veil of will
A Master Puppeteer

86

In quiet whispers
Thou art adorned
In mirthful silence
Thou art felt
In mellow radiance
Thou art revealed

87

Hours with Thee
In silence
Seems
Like a wink
In the face of Time

88

In body's aloneness
I prepare
Soul's union
With Thee

89

Sisters twin
Tears and Laughter
Joy conceived
At creation's dawn
One nectared unburdening
The other
Musical outpouring
Man's loftiest praise
To Divinity's dramatic play

90

Anything that brings Bliss
Cannot be sin
Bliss
An ego cessation
Timeless
Holy
A gratitude prayer
Its flesh vehicle
Trivial not
Or enemy
It's a masterpiece
Of intricate generosity
For mortal
To play God
For a moment

91

When thy tears
Pierce
The prism of His will
There will be a cloudburst
A spectrum
Of a million hues

92

Maiden Karma
Blindfolded and just
Weighs in her scales
Cause effect anew
Neither cries
Or bribes
Touch her heart impartial
Till a child free
Climbs her knee
Pulls the rag darkened
Wonder and relief
Enters the bosom stoned
Scales fall
Deafening clamour
Mother gathers
Into hungry numbed arms
Forgiven the mathematics
Of innumerable births
From bee to Brahma

93

It is not cursed wombs
That birth maimed minds
A mind all heart
A heart that knows no mind
No womb is cursed
None that transforms
A spark to flame
Feeding its own blood
Cursed is that flame
Which burns
When sent it was
To warm

94

The frozen heart lake
Melts
Memory birds come
After a long winter sleep
To dive
Catch fish
Shaken awake
By hungry bird cries

95

Chaotic despair
Seeps through
Every fibre of my being
As my pristine self
Watches the struggle
With trifles
While the seed of Thy wish
For Thee in me
Takes root
Branches out
But bears not
Fruit or flower
For the hungry birds
Intoxicated bees

96

Evil seeds
Carried like potent pollen
Through lush incarnational fields
Sprout
Germinate
Spread
In young freshly ploughed lives
Words of the wise
Passion of concerned love
Fail to roast
The demonic seedlings

97

I shall walk away
Without a backward glance
And break into a wild run
At the sight of Thy castle spheres
Beyond the sunless forest
Of this swamped existence

98

Joy fireworks
Burn to cinders
Accumulated pain clouds
From the hearts
Of men
And nations

99

Solitude
Glides
Through empty expanse
Of Thy temple
While Silence
Unadorned
Dry eyed
Sighs
In a barren regret

100

A yawning emptiness
Stares
Unblinking
Into the abyss
Of my God empty soul

101

When blood
Retains in veins
Hope there is
To purify
But once spilt on dust
Is trampled on
Even blued red
Trifled brown

102

Thy will
Impregnates
Every desire seed
To its blossoming
In the bower
Of our silence

103

In trifled moments
I but throw away
An eternity
With Thee

104

The ark of my being
Sways
In Thy vast oceanic mind
Why need I fear
Crashing waves?
When Thou my Captain
And my heart the compass
That points always
Towards the horizon
Of Thy grace

105

When my noble five
Are at Thy service
Can't the hundred foster ones
Of unknown parentage
Be made thy slaves
To be whipped
And crushed
Before coronation day?

106

In fatigued unruliness
Lay unbuilt
The bridge
That connects
My famined shore
To Thy
Love drenched oasis

107

Thou hast given us
The freedom
To clip our wings
And stutter
A broken song
In caged karma
Or feed
On Thy word
Grow wings afire
That melt iron bars
For a swift
Heavenly flight

108

I watch unflustered
As bruised souls
Walk stealthily
In a world
Strewn with shattered glass
I smile
As mercurial souls
Embrace
To strangle
I weep
As eagle souls
Clip wings
To cajole caged ravens

109

The serpent stirs
But Thy love's thunderbolt
Crushes it
Hood and all

110

A quiet dread
Squeezes
My heart
As if to empty it
Of Thy grace

111

A dream buried
May sprout
In climes another
A plant poison
Set free
May return
With fledglings anew
But surrendered
Will triumph
Riding atop
Shoulders giant
Though a vision
Pygmied

112

In devotion's lair
Are reared
Lion cubs
Of fearlessness

113

Ice melts
Freezing fire
Knifed pain
Rusts even gold

114

Beyond the spheres
Of Darkness and Light
We soar
On wings afire
Where a million suns
Laugh galaxies
And blinded Time
Chained in a cave dark
Surrenders
His wretched tyranny

115

Most whimper
Their abject submission
Others cringe
At thine indifferent disdain
Some shake thee
By the throat
Until thou retch out
Thy green ire
A blessed few
Toss thou in the air
Joyous jugglery
Of pleasures met
Hungers fed
Whistling on
Without a glance backward
At thy crumbling soil

116

Lament not
When you go
Flaming tailed meteors
Will be the pall bearers
Crashing forests
Thy pyre
A lightening bolt
Blue and pure
Will ignite it
And a storm torrential
To the hungry ocean
Carry the ashes sacred

117

Thou art untying
All the knots
Even though in impatience
We hold Thy Hands
And hinder
The working
Of Thy charming pattern

118

What suffers
The mind or the body?
Or the death
Of hope?
The flowering
Of decayed seeds
Planted in the shade
Of a heart mighty?
Or a will to live
For to want to die
Is blasphemy?

119

The hands that embraced
Were nailed to the cross
A life divine
That breathed on Thy will
Hung bleeding
Forsaken
If obedience
Retribution brings
Nature justly shelters Her children
With Ignorance
Like a wise helpless mother
From the ambitions
Of a father stern

120

From the crest of grace
I gave a joy call
And Thou responded
In undying echoes of the same
And when I threw a pebble
Huge boulders crashed down
In a precarious stream of venom
When I give Thee to the world
Thou jump back from a million arms
Like a hungry infant
Plucked from the mother's bosom
Longs for the nectared warmth

121

What is this magic?
I laugh the quiet
Laughter of liberation
When around me
Fly spears of wrath
What is this mystery?
I bellow in fiery indignation
When one oversteps the line
Between concern and curse

122

Every atom
Of my love soul
I stuffed
With the ragged cloth
Of disillusionment
Lest they cry out
In a million tongues
Love's lost dreams
But my simmering passion
Might ignite
In any clime
An inferno for Thee

123

What made this numbness
That looks on serene?
An inner quiet
Untouched by panic
Is it indifference
To a pain scarred face?
Or a gradual collapse
Of the heart's resilience?
Or is it Thy play
To merge the actor
And the audience
In one compassionate sweep
Of stilled Timelessness?

124

Thou sent the scroll
Thy messenger mounts
The swift white steed
The burnished gold sword
Shines in the mellow light
The ancient guest waits
Once more
Impatient and adorned
With Thy sacred Word
The old tattered cloak
Slips away
And Thou throws
A luminous one
Star studded
Plucked from Thy Heart garden

125

A shift
In consciousness
Wrought by Thy grace
Numbed
Detached
Awed
Silenced
To meet
The dark cloaked
Luminous guest
Who frees
Breaks open
The nailed window
To help escape
Into infinite wilderness

126

When was that unguarded
Ominous moment
For a crystallized drop
Of poisonous pain
To cut through
The unarmed heart
And pierce the fortified soul?
That eerie moment
Which sent a tremor
Through sleeping galaxies
To cajole back
A faithful reflection
From its empty earth sojourn?

127

Death comes
With heavy thumping footsteps
To one terrified
And crouched in a corner
Or a faithful lover is He
Climbing a flower creeper
On a moonless night
Into the hungry embrace
Of one imprisoned in a tower dingy
Or She is a Mother
Who frets to see Her child
Wallowing in mud
Washes him
In a river of light
To clothe and bedeck
And slip into
The Hands of the proud Father

128

The Divine Doctor
Sugar coats bitter pills
For terrified reluctant little ones
For others
He might hold the nose
Until breathless
Gulped down in huge gasps
Or opens a vein
And forces in drop by drop
Sometimes a painful prick
Agonizing in anticipation
Than the deed
But for some
He cuts
Scrapes
Scalds
Gnawing out cemented wrongs
And when all exhausted
Feeds Her
Who fed
To fashion new clay
A new temple
For the Guest Divine

129

I embraced
My anger
And the whining
Fretful child
Whimpered itself
To sleep

130

The ancient
Poisoned shaft
Simmering
In my Joy self
Thou pulled out
With a mighty thrust
And cupped my mouth
With a love glance
Lest the scream
Drown the stars
In cosmic fires

131

My bleeding stumps
Have healed
I've sprouted wings
Pinions of burnished gold
That catch Thy fiery light
Thy wounded warrior has awakened
From the nightmare of defeat
Bring me the delusion mercenaries
Thy warrior's sword is ready
And his wings quiver in impatience
For the mighty righteous war

132

It's not justice
But perfectly unjust love
That governs this universe
Justice is mechanical
A pull of the string
And the universe whirrs
Chugs along in succession
What role then for that Artist
Who bends over His work
Shivering and starved
To correct a tiny flaw
In the farthest corner
Of His giant canvas?
It's love that makes a grass blade
Aspire to touch the sun
And a tree to hide its nut
Beneath the earth
For the mother squirrel

133

I stabbed my pain
With laughter
And tears gushed forth
Like the Old Faithful

134

Should I remove the thorn
With a thorn?
Or let fleshed Time
Camouflage wrong
And limp along?
Or surrender the hardened poison
To take root
In my soul garden
To sprout a grace blossom
On every deadly spear?

135

Adversity is wasted
If it fails
To make one
Fearless
Compassionate
Let the gods
Knead
Fresh clay
After every
Dishonoured destiny

136

At life's betrayals
I flew
In caged attachment
And fell
Wounded
Broken winged
Now I stand
At the edge
Of the well
As the drowned moon
Beckons
A silver plunge

137

Life will not
Stop me from living
With magnetized spine
Dignified eyes
I lift disaster by the collar
And hurl him face down
Into oblivion's pit
Dusting my fingers
I call on more
Only to see the cowards
Clambering in hasty retreat
Into minds ungraced by Thee

138

The dark night of the soul
Is over
The Bird of Paradise gently stirs
Dawn is playfully
Nudged awake
The rose meadows
Impatiently await bloom
And the lotus pond
Smiles her invitation
To happy naked children

139

As I reached
To pluck the honeyed fruit
I slipped on the razor's edge
Whole night my soul
Lay bleeding
While my flesh
Slumbered in defiance
At dawn
Thou gently drew back
Delusion's curtain
And lovingly bathed my wounds
As though it was not I
Who had left Thy clasp
But Thou who allowed
Me to stray

140

I am a corpse
Unmoving
Unfeeling
On my pyre
In the burning ghat
Of this world
The skulls of my dreams
Scattered lay
As Thou light the fire
That awakens
To life everlasting

141

Thy call to duty shows
My wounds have healed
Slowly I put on
My armour
Sharpen my sword
But tarry
Lest Thou may
Call me back to Thee
To applaud and bless
As life marches past
In a procession of triumph

142

I crawled
In the shadow
Of the serpent's claws
Now I soar
In the shade
Of the eagle's wings

143

Now I know
Why Thy heart
Followed Judas
With a painful tenderness
For he made Thee
See Thy shining face
In the blood lake
Of Thy wound
Dragging Thee closer
To Heaven's gates
Maimed
Broken
Bleeding
But sprouting wings
Ready
For the final flight

144

Should I pray like a tempest
Shaking the gods out of their stupor?
Or be a gentle stream
Washing Their feet in service
And wait with folded palms
Bowed head
For a nugget?
Or offer myself as a house of prayer
All in surrender echoing Thee?
The stone of my little self
Needs to bleed under Thy chisel
I am Thy work
Thou decide the manner
Place
Time
Paralyze my hands
Lest they direct Thine
For the colossal transformation
From stone to soul

145

When a mother
Stumbles
Even gods
Rush in
To ease
The fall

146

What sorrow
For the plough
That pulls out
The entrails
Of Earth mother?
For the Farmer
Knows the way
And the seasons

147

Sweet cushion
To day's labour
Blissful drowning
In forgetfulness's bosom
Gentle caress
On Time's wrinkled brow
Honeyed whispers
On moon filled nights
Trembling lips
On volcanic heartbeats
O Sleep! Winged enchantress
Bury me in Thy deep embrace

148

A whiff of maddening fragrance
From some long forgotten meadow
A flash of eerie lightening
On a cloud impregnated sky
The song of a lone bird
Quivering a spring burst tree
A drop of nectared rain
On a desert parched mouth
A touch of cold steel
On a dream invested heart
Is the memory of one
Pulled too soon
Unto the Mother's embrace

149

When Pain dips her sore finger
In shallow sense pond
Addictions bubble up
When she enters mind river
Madness manifests
But when soul ocean
Drags her in
Blinded
Choked
Numbed
Limbs tied
Fate rock around neck
Sinks
Then an upsurge
A gasping for breath
Pain metamorphoses
To Art
A plea
For breaths few
Rewarded
An elixir of life

150

That lone tear
Which wells
From the heart ocean
Thou catch
On Thy Finger
And gently slip
Into Time's oystered shell
To transform
Brined hurt into
A pearly harvest

151

No
The Wound
Is not healed
Just a drop
Of the old venom
And it festers
Boils
Erupts
The Wound
Shrouded
Mocks
Patience
Pretence
Howls
To be heard
The Wound
Will walk
To the pyre
And roar
In ecstasy
Embracing
The naked flames
The Wound
May smile
In another
Incarnation's wisdom

152

Beloved Mother
In the long famine of failure
Thou ceaselessly plough
The hard crust of my soul
While Father scatters generously
Wisdom seeds
My repentance tears mingle
With Thy holy sweat
To sprout tender greens
In the arid tracts
Dark karma clouds
Melt in a gentle drizzle
At the warmth
Of my Master's presence
Come thunder and lightning
Flood my being
In a mighty spate
Till soil and green vanish
Into the vast upsurge of the sea

153

Tie my wild colt
Of free will
With Thy wisdom rope
Lest it dash
Its tiny blind brain
On delusion walls
Ride it
Though saddle less
With Thy firm will
And gallop away
Into the orange horizon
In a cloud
Of holy dust

154

With heavy eyes
Unsteady spine
Strays barking
At the midnight moon
I implore Thee
To my vacant heart
Come Mother Divine
Of a million hugs
Pour Thy Joy
Into every pore
Of my Bhakti starved being

155

In dark death valleys
I stumble on
Led by the nose
By my tyrant little will
Now I give Thee
The reins
Also a whip
To lead me
Out of delusion valleys
Into the mountain top
Of celestial light

156

Thou chiselled my dross
With Thy iron hammer
Now Thou hast reached
The uncut diamond of my being
Gently Thou art at work
Diamond shaping diamond
The twinkle in Thine eyes
Mingle with my tears
Forming a rainbow path
For this little one
To run into
Thy waiting bosom

157

At Thy touch
Evaporates
Incarnations
Of crusted pain

158

Iron out the creases
That Thou may emboss
The intricate pattern
Of Thy will
On the silken purple
Of my eternal being

159

Thou touched me
And the burnt rope
Of desire bondage
Crumbled away
Then Thou plucked
The morning star
And embossed it
On my naked forehead
Deep crusted fate lines
Furrowed with misery incarnating seeds
Seeds rooted banyan like
Tremble at the distant roar
Of the tempest
The mighty spate of many waters
That will drown the three worlds
Of this tiny twilight lamp
To float
In Thy tranquil thought lake

160

A dream laughter river
Washed away
Anger stains
From the pristine satin
Of my being

161

My unshed tears
Crystallized into Thy holy linga
In my dark soul cave
Aeons passed
Then a shaft
Of Thy mercy light
Pierced through
A crevice
Melting the hallowed ice
Bathing my being
With a perennial
Mountain spring

162

Thy divine cow of plenty
Tied at delusion's post
With attachment rope
Devours sense debris
Until Thou whispered
A sweet counsel
To chew on the rope
And bound away
Into the green pastures
Of an eternal freedom

163

You lay coiled
In earth's wombal fire
While I waited
Stilled breath
In iced Himalayan wilderness
Till a lone Grace tear
Aeons chiselled
Cut through thy slumber
And planted a Joy seed
For infinity's love play

164

The storm has receded
The fruit garden
Lays uprooted
And the wounded earth
Awaits Thy flower seeds
To fill
Her vacant womb

165

I scattered
Desire seeds
In a valley of flame
Now the bitter crop
Is ready for harvest
Send Thou
A mercy tornado
To destroy
The poison plants

166

Drenched in Thy love
Karmic fires
Do not pain
Like matchsticks
Soaked in rain

167

Every desire
Undeserved
Every joy
Unearned
Reaped
Harvested
In the pain
Of some great love
What poison
Thou my Shiva Guru
Drinks smiling
In my wish
For enlightenment nectar?

168

The dark clouds
Have receded
The sky is clear
For Thee to splash
Thy million grace hues

169

I won't be tucked in
For a long warm sleep
Attend to this
Wet whimpering waif
Lest my screams
Shatter the Maya induced sleep
Of Thy drugged children
Carry me as Thou hustle along
Thy cosmic chores
No more rocking cradles
Or toys for me
No more Father's veiled karmic threats
Or the gentle imploring of the Nurse
I want Thee
My lovely Mother
Tied as I am to Thee
By a million umbilical cords

170

Incessantly I've asked Thee
Thy will
In whispers hoarse
And loud
My doubts have often sold Thee
For thirty brazen pieces of silver
But now when I climb
Calvary with my cross
I see the cross
Is Thy will
Deaf to jeering crowds
Leaden weight
I hug
Kiss it
With bleeding mouth
Until the cross and I
Are nailed
Each to each
In a perfect crucifixion
Of surrender to Thee

171

In the tug of war
Of breath and I
Who cuts
The bleeding rope?

172

As worlds crash
Around me
Thou turn it
Into a symphony
Of Thy approach

173

It's blasphemy
To say I love
When all I am
Is a channel
For Thine all conquering love
To flow through
An infinite breathing
From every pore of creation
Plant
Stone
Planets
An unending giving
And receiving
From Thee to Thee

174

Was I the stone
On which Thy blood rained?
The thorn
That crowned Thee?
The bread
That fed hungry multitudes?
The whip
That lashed Thee?
The water
That washed Thy holy feet?
The one who betrayed?
Or the one who watched over
Thy form beloved
In the sepulchre cold?

175

Quietly
Thou wash away
Layers of clogged realities
For the Truth
To shine
In detached glory

176

Thou traced
With fingers fiery
My furrowed fate line
Entrenched deep
From west to east
On a care wrinkled forehead
Buried it deep
In a blazing circle
End consumed
By beginning
Like a chant sacred
Whispered atop a mountain
Carried by the breeze
To the topmost pine
And the humble valley reed

177

In the harsh summer heat
Blows Thy cool
Hope breeze
Like a nest readied
On the loftiest branch
For lost nomadic birds
As they fly home
On weary wings
Cooled by rain drenched clouds

178

Should I knock
On ingratitude's
Indifferent door
And extend
A hand wounded
To a dagger yielding one?
Or plant my rose bush
As the sun slowly
Climbs the high mountains
To shine on Thy temple dewed?

179

When Karma lashed
With her thorn whip
Thou rushed in
Taking blows
Shielding shocks
But Thy sacred blood
Splashed and flowed
In rivulets fragrant
Bathing fever
Quenching thirst
Of every wronged
Atom of my being

180

Earth
In hunger
Wailed
Heaven
Tore open
Nectared bosom

181

I accept
With arms open
Thy verdict
But my heart
Shudders
At the weight
Of Thy gift

182

In the bliss brimmed eyes
Of a sage
I bathed
Infinite
Mercy baths

183

When the Master Surgeon
Cut open the body
And stitched up
The cleansed part
He put the knife
On another
Readied for repair
What use protests
Or muffled moans
When the Surgeon
Dons the robe?

184

I have noticed
Thou art kinder
After I err
Gentle with the wounded
No wonder
The villains
Have it so good

185

I am a Mother
Spared the pangs of birth
Nightly vigils over feverish brows
Steep climbs to boon bestowing shrines
I am a Mother
To the bird the insect
The twig the flower
The stone the mountain
The ocean the ditch
I am a Mother
Trembling in the passion of my need
As you mingle the earth and the seed
They gather the joyous harvest
While I the scarecrow wither in the sun
I am a Mother
As I point to the broken spine
The dragging foot the frozen brain
The heavenly voyager the sad clown
The orphaned bully
I am a Mother
As You shake Your head
You who quiver at the fall of a sparrow
Walk on toes lest it hurt an ant
Will not contain the pain
You be a river
Quenching playing delighting
Rushing towards the Ocean
The Mother

186

On the banks of Her
Who had drowned Her sons
We sat ready to immerse our cravings
For a flesh of our blood
Thou tended the holy fire
While we dipped our beings in Her
Into the raging flames
With tears silent we threw them
The last crumbs of our desires
The final soot of incarnations
We are free
We are free
If ever
It will be Thy will
Never the plea of our blind self

187

If a tree am I
My father beloved the root
Digging deep into my soul
Gripping with attachment
Divine Woodcutter
I see Thy approach
My every leaf trembles
In the whirlwind of Thy strides
In surrender
I hand Thee the axe
Fashioned from my wood
Thy touch turns it to gold
I shut my million eyes
As Thou get ready to strike
The eerie silence prolongs
Gently I open my eyes to Thy smile
Thy work is done
I lay on the ground
But there was no pain
Only an anticipation of agony
That too evaporates
As Thou collect the roots
As faggots for Thy sacrifice
Soon the sun shall do his work
The rest of me will wilt and dry
To be ready for Thy holy fire

188

My heart contracts in compassion
For the disillusioned wrongdoer
Was it plan or pain
That prompts such outbursts?
Thy hand tight in mine
I look on
With tear brimmed eyes
One more lighthouse of hope
Crashes into the sea

189

The fragrant
Camphor fire
Of Thy will
Leaves
No karmic residue

190

Make complete
This surrender
That fear vultures
Find no carrion of doubt
In the flower meadows
Of my evergreen faith

191

Stretch me
To my form cosmic
That I embrace Thee
In every atom
Of infinite universes

192

Thou poured Thy love
Over young thirsty souls
As my motherhood yearned
To embrace all
In a timeless moment
As perhaps Thou too ached
In climes past
For one just Thine
The call of blood for blood
In a sea of myriad salt

193

East star
Has risen
In a moonburst
Of royal blue
And aeons of crucifixion
Wiped away
In showers of light

194

Serpentine resentments
Coil around soul
Stifling pristine breath
Of peace whispers
Be Thou the lone star
That guides out
Of this viper pit
Crawling with venomous
Entanglements

195

When painful apathy
Overwhelms
Thou counsel
To see One in all
To be all
The maid
Who shines the floor
For crowds
To imprint with muddied footsteps
The leader
In vacuumed coolness
The sun baked
Information dispensers
Joyless
Drowsy eyed
Shuffling toward month ends

196

Thou held
In a loving embrace
And all fears
Melted away
Like hardened ice
Under the foot
Of the sun
A wind whipped glacier
In the mouth of a volcano

197

Thou hold firm
My mind reins
Lest the wild steeds
Break bounds
Escape
Into the wilderness
Though bleeding
Bruised
Torn
Limping

198

My love
A storm tossed sprout
Finds root
In my ancient
Weed cleared
Heart garden
And Thou Master Gardener
Keeps a vigil eternal
For twig
To blossom temple

199

I played my part
As Thy child
Thou withheld
Father like
I'm hurt
But Thou knowest
The nature of fire
And wood
Still my heart cringes
Sulks
Scolds
At my own deception

200

In my empty
Heart chalice
Pour Thou but a drop
Of Thy love wine
And it will froth
Overflow
Inundate
My parched barren being

201

Thou caressed
My wilting countenance
As though rare alabaster
And joy blossoms
Sprung from every pore
While the world
Tore open
Vandalized
My unpainted brow
And found
A tomb
Crumbling temple
Of festering tears

202

Thou sharpen
The dagger
And Thou alone
Make it blunt
In this Thy will's see saw
Smiles the Witness above

203

The weary night wails
Laboured with pregnant dawn
Groans the eclipsed moon
Heavy with unmilked light
When She
Heaven's Midwife
Stumbles to assist
Yet another birth
Breathing prayers
Washing stains
That cling
On knotted wrinkles
Bows in reverence
At emerging light
Blood scorched
Pain released
Unburdened fruit
On trembling palms
Not death crimsoned
Like the butcher's
But saffroned
In yet another birth

204

I searched for Thee
Like one lost
In the carnival
Of a foreign land
They speak not our tongue
Nor hug as tight
Their reddened smiles
Tear at my heart
In the wombs of these caricatures
All I received
Were chains that bind
A burning note
Of pleasure debts
Endured
Than celebrated

205

What price
The wombal rent?
The seed
That sanctified soil
The soil
That gave space
A receiving
In giving
Then why
This rent?
A mercenary badge
On a martyr's
Thorn crown?

206

In the peace stilled
Heartlake
I gazed
At Thy God eloquent eyes
And like Narcissus of yore
Slipped from Time's eternal grasp
For crimsoned flesh to flower
A pristine fragrant white

207

Thou splashed rainbow hues
On the cosmic canvas
To create a masterpiece
For eternity's recall
Two souls sculpted
To be one
Perfected in myriad strokes
Of distinct togetherness
Once a babe
Suckling on the bosom of service
Roles reversed in another Time
The cherub now the mother
Cascading parental debt
Milked blood flows
Through sibling veins
Joyous playmates
Confidante close
Then the lovers

Prized possessions each
Intense amber poetry
Burning through nervous veins
At the end of the soul's sojourn
A lull
An earned peace
A symphony of love shades
An unstained mirror
Reflecting God's own blush
The two become one
Friends
The seer and seen alike

208

The caged bird
Flutters her broken wings
As the Bird of Paradise
Looks nonchalantly on
What meaning a palace
Or a hovel dingy
When the luminous blue
Sweeps through the slits
But never a magic carpet
To soar over promised lands
Or perch on the gentle shoulder
Of the Messiah
As He scatters
Wisdom seeds
In the town square

209

In Thine embrace
The dramatic play
Of all
Appears like a drop
Of momentary water
On a lotus leaf
Touches
But does not wet
Falls
But does not emboss

210

Thou may ignore
My transparent tears
Silent sighs
But not my bleeding footsteps
As I walk through
My shattered heart
Into Thy marble palace

211

With Thy dagger of love
Clip the wings
Of my airy ambitions
To perch on Thy shoulder
As the world marches by
In a symphony of triumph

212

Beloved
On the shores of eternity
Let us hold hands
And watch
As our souls crash head on
And shatter
Into a million twinkling stars

213

I pleased
Ever vigilant senses
Often bartering blood
Unresponsive ties
Unknown masses
But now
In the midst of
Cluttered shattered fancies
I heard Thy gentle whisper
Just please Me
And my soul stood still
Like a tree hit by lightening
On a storm tossed night
Stripped of the burden
Of a million green claws
Cindered
But blazing in the dark

214

I thank Thee
For the tears
As they made Thy gentle hands
Touch my face
Laughter would have brought
Just an echo
But the tears
Brought Thy touch

215

If life is a romance divine
Between Thee and I
Why do Thee
Wait so patiently
For this coquette
Who attends to all
The frivolous
And the serious
But is exhausted
Inattentive
In Thy loyal presence?

216

As Thou hast truly loved
Through the steady flame
Of my eternal love
I believe Thou alone will
Pour Thy distilled oil
To keep the fire aflame

217

The sunshine
Of Thy smile
Eclipsed Thy pain
Like an exiled prince
Refuses to bow
To an upstart usurper
Even as the goblet of death
Is sanctified by a royal kiss

218

With the fiery rays
Of my timeless love
I pierced through
Thine alluring smile
And my eyes overflowed
As my heart dam broke
At Thy compassionate deception

219

Thou came disguised
In forms varied
But Thine eyes
Smiling in an ageless love
Gave Thyself away

220

Thou art teasing me
With masks grey
And colourful
But behind the clamour
In tiny discreet moments
I catch a glimpse
Of that auric smile
And my heart whistles
A tune gay
At the unfolding of Thy play

221

In the winter
Of my soul I long
For Spring's song bird
To crack open
My frozen heart
With the warmth
Of a lost love song

222

Thy hand touched
My blazing forehead
And I mock
The stars
That chained me
With invisible rays
No more ransomed time
Walking on eggshells
When Thou beckons
Through the corridors of Heaven
To race into
Thine outstretched arms

223

One
Binds
All
Frees
What grief
The courtesan
Whose heart door
Ajar remain?
While the chaste wife
Pines the night
For drunken footsteps

224

At solitude's beckoning
I tiptoe
Into Thine embrace
Mesmerized
To find
All my loves
Etched on Thy face

225

Thou parted
My trembling mud
With Thy ruby
And words
Flew out
On honeyed wings

226

Thou sharpened
Thy love knife
On my
Stone heart
Until it
Cracked
Bled
Inundating universes

227

As I stood
Selling my wares
In the busy marketplace
Thou rode in
On a lightening steed
And as the crowds gasped
Shielding eyes
From the euphoric light
Thou pulled me
To Thy massive heart
Locking trembling mouths
In a final stamp
Of Thy possession

228

Today when lovers
Clink glasses
Of their immortal longings
I raise mine
To solitude
That feared moor
On a moonless night
When the echoes
Of one's footsteps
Collide with the prayerful
Thumping of the heart
On such a dark night
Of my expectant soul
I raised a toast
To myself

229

I dip
But the tip of a finger
And the love wine
Bubbles in mirth
What drunken madness
Awaits
When we'll drown
The last drop
And smash
The fragile chalice
Into the fragrant fire?

230

Tonight
My soul
Whirls in bliss
Leaving an ache
As my earth shoe
Pinches
Sprains
But with the music's
Quickening beat
I shall kick off
The leathered impediment
And sink bare feet
Into creation's bosom

231

Thy prodigal friend
Gate crashed
Into Thy palatial heart
Only to find Thee
Waiting
With one foot poised
Over the dance floor
And a goblet
Of an ancient love wine
Extended in welcome

232

A lone star
Keeps vigil
In midnight's sky
For one to sprout wings
On a leaden form

233

Thou whose home
Is the splendour of creation
Came to my little temple
In the corner of obscurity

234

Thou refused
The golden keys
To Thy sacred
Heart chamber
I sulked
In rejection
When sweetly
Thou whispered
Locked doors
Inaccessible vaults
Need keys
But for thee
My love
No doors guard
The dark fragrant
Forgotten niche
Where on a loveseat
Waits
Thy heavy eyed Prince

235

In the land
Beyond breath
We shall meet
And churn
Love's ether
In a new
Understanding

236

Am I Thy favourite
Among little ones infinite?
I asked Thee
As we swayed
In the rose meadows
Thou smiled and said
Which among these blossoms
Is thy love?
All watered and cared
Rainbow hued
Gentle loves
But this one
Red and small
Dug into
My buttonhole
I care with
My heart blood
Plucked from its brethren
Rootless and thirsty
I feed
With My life blood

237

Once again
Time lifts
The bridal veil
Will I blush
And bite trembling lips?
Or lock
Lioned gaze
And waltz
On winged feet
Across the heavens?

238

In midnight's stillness
I await Thy knock
On the door
Of my peace

239

My spinal cross
Will bloom
Into the dazzling lotus
Of Thy grace
From earth water fire air ether
Through the dark forest of delusion
Petal by petal
Breath chiseled
In the sapphire Om lake
It will bloom
My cross
A scepter
For the Prince of peace
On His bliss throne
To gaze on
His kingdom cosmic

240

Breathe into my spine flute
Thine heavenly music
And all my senses
Shall rush
Like bliss intoxicated damsels
Into Thine opal presence

241

In my silent soul corridor
I await
Thy tinkling footsteps
A gentle breeze
Lets in the sunlight
Through curtained darkness
And I who am restless
In all waiting
Wait for Thee
With the calm
Of an oak
Shedding yellowed leaves
For the inevitable spring

242

Thou came
Robed in blue
With a casket
Of liquid peace

243

When will Thou come?
My Rabboni
With molten eyes of tranquil love
I breathe and bade time
In the shattering
Picking up pieces
Of innumerable loves
But my heart waits
Poised as an arrow
In the taunt bow
Of a blinded marksman

244

The ancient
Intense eyes
I sought
Were Thine

245

I lamented
There was no flower
In my crystal vase
When a wild wind
Blew off the shut windows
Of my heart cottage
I lived
In the midst
Of Thy rose meadows

246

All my desire toys
Will be abandoned
When the thought
Of our betrothal
Strikes
My Father fond

247

Through a veil
Of unshed
Heart tears
I mistake
Every form
To be Thine

248

Drenched
In Thy molten light
I bloom
In an eternal Spring

249

Inundated
In Thy love
I caress all
With my
Indulgent eyes

250

Blue eyed heaven
Gazed lovelorn
At colourless ocean
And she blushes
In kind
As Thy whispering
Longing look
From every star and flower
Fills a heart vanquished
With thirsts unknown

251

Thou dragged me
Wailing
Protesting
To the summit
And pushed
For faith wings
To sprout
Now I sprint up
For a renunciation dive
Into Thy Bliss Ocean

252

Tear out
My pond heart
Stagnant
Vile
Into a love ocean
For Thee to drown
And surface
Quenched
Surfeited
Of creation

253

The serpent stirred
At the temple's threshold
As the seven deities
Lay awake in slumber
And the divine monkey
Atop the highest citadel
Swayed drunk with Thy name

254

When love
Surfeits
As anger
Nature chuckles
In permissive patience
Like a lover
Receives blows
On his bosom bare
Wonders at the hardness
Of that palm
That melts butter like
When his finger tips
Brush past it
In a deliberate accident

255

None have embraced me
Drunk with spring madness
Nor traced the course
Of tears to source
Poetry of the blushing moon
Music of singing streams
Imprisoned
In chambers secret
Of a heart juvenile
For Thee to woo
Breathe fragrance
Of an untouched lotus
With a thousand
Tender petals

256

Thou hast gently shut
Our bridal chamber
And the noise and cares
Of this dream world
Fade away

257

I send Thee a fervent love note
Urgent and rare
Come in Thy wedding finery
And whisk me away
Long have I played coquette
To imposters wanton
Lust
Anger
Greed
Dignity devoid
Unbecoming of one
Royal betrothed
Let the world know
From the arms of the Mother
I eloped
With the Emperor

258

Today I felt
Thy silent shadow
Shining on my every deed
Until in reckless abandon
I crushed Thy form
In a mischievous misstep

259

When love
Disappoints
I knock
At Thy door
And find
Closed
It never was

260

When I lean
But a little
Towards old
Familiar loves
Thou pull me back
With a jerk wild
Into Thine eternal embrace

261

In dance divine
I shed the snake skin
Of shame
As Thou stirred
My blood
With the madness
Of cosmic drum beats

262

Thou made me discard
The last piece
Of silken garment
From my God shy self
That I may come
Unfettered
Unchained
For Thine embrace

263

My desires come
Gaudily dressed grooms
One on a high restless steed
Another on an ass docile
And yet another on foot
Heart palpitating
Eyes uneasy
I sieve the horizon
For Thee
I would rather remain
Unadorned
Unwed
Than take the hand of another
Who promises a kingdom
But surrenders not his heart
I long for Thee
My guileless Bridegroom
With Thee a corner
In this mighty world
Is all I crave

264

I dance
In the azure orb
Of Thy grace
Throat choked
Tears suspended
All you need from me
Is my all
To it will Thou add
Thine all

265

Lived eternity
In a moment
Of stillness poised
Flesh my holy stallion
Quenched its thirst
In waters turbulent
Race on
Refreshed anew
Thy goal that summit
That blind plunge
Into the fire dried lake
To stretch a moment
To eternity unbroken

266

In love's stillness
My soul
Gazes at Thee
Ages pass
Fish turns to man
Man to superman
As silence
Merges into silence
In silence

267

I was a girl little
In my father's home
Content with dolls and baubles
One day they gave me
Thy image divine
With promises
Of pleasures unknown
Night and day
I awaited Thee
My dolls thrown forlorn
In a corner
Hungrily I listened
To tales of Thy glory
And lit a lamp
On my nightly vigil
I find no interest
In the calls of my playmates
Nor do I hear
The gallop of Thy steed
I am lost
Suspended in mid stream
Of them who laugh
Wonder at my lunacy
And Thee who think me
Unworthy of claim

268

Through Thy love drenched eyes
I see me
And blush
In eternal youthfulness

269

In passion's lair
I rolled
On blossom beds
Singing Thy praise
Who gave
Fragrance to colour
Light to matter

270

Thou planted
A rose garden
Amidst a thorn fence
And the song birds came
Though the night is dark

271

Thou showered tributes
Like a mid summer
Torrential storm
While I stood drenched
To the bones
With a soul smile
That lit up the heavens

272

Thy voice flowed
Rich ancient honey
Up my spine
Offering oblations
To bliss intoxicated gods

273

If He sends
The Pain
Won't He give
A Laughter vessel
To collect it?

274

As the years
Sink
Into the saffron horizon
I see Thy hope vessel
Rowing furiously
Towards me

275

In lunacy's freedom
I roll naked
On burning sands
Chase terrified gulls
In wild laughter
Hang fish and crabs
On wind tangled tresses
Suckle dolphins
On love brimmed bosom
And in the crimsoned sunset
Await my Bridegroom
On the canopy
Of crashing waves

276

I fed
My soul hunger
With sweetened
Thoughts of Thee

277

From my life wound
Grows Thy love lotus
And the intoxicated bee mind
Unmindful of the tyrant queen
Lingers past the light
To be embraced
Into the petaled warmth
Of honeyed oblivion

278

When tears
Turn disloyal
And refuse to shed
On blood marked days
Be Thou the lover
Who unearths
The sweetest secret
That prayed
For this wound
This thorned rose
Beautiful
Reddened
With martyred blood

279

Thou touched
The shimmering blue
Of my mind lake
With the dew
Of Thy grace
And the wind
Which came to sigh
Lingered
With a song

280

In the crystal vase
Of my expectant heart
Is the distilled
Holy waters
Of myriad rivers
Ready
For Thy blossoms

281

I throw
But a pebble
Into Thy vast
Shoreless mind lake
But its ripples
Will pull
At Thy taut
Heartstrings

282

I shall flaunt
My scars
Love bites from Thee
No ointments rare
Surgeons clever
Can erase
One marked by Thee

283

Gold winged bird
Thy will fashioned
One light soars
In innumerable loves
Of pristine little hearts
The other lead drops
In harsh homed loves
Between soaring and crashing
My soul laughs
In the infinite blue

284

In Thine arms
I've tasted
Laughter's joyous pain
Tear's painful joy

285

Thou I love
Is destiny's design
But how much
Is my will free

286

Presence
Of absence
Seeps through
Every pore
Until
Onion like
Rind after rind
Plucked away
Arrives Absence
Torrents in
Uprooting doors
Swallows emptiness
Into the Emptiness
Absence
Embraces absence
In Presence

287

It's been a long time
Though a tiny dent in eternity
This waiting
In the dark
To make the first move
I've scrubbed the pots and pans
Thou hast created a few more galaxies
But our nocturnal embraces
Are cold and silent
Daylight finds me again
At the bathing ghat
Hiding from my sniggering sisters
Another miscarried destiny

288

The heart vessel
Scrubbed clean
Of attachment dirt
To pour
The milk of Thy will
For the final oblations
As Thou hold
My trembling little palms
Over Arunachala Linga

289

Thou hast given me
The morning star
And the delusion night
Melts in an abyss
Of endless light

290

Volcanic avalanches
That claw out
The entrails
Of a mother
Heavy with child
A love
That licks
Leprous wounds
Like scarlet honey
Wild haired lunacy
Howling pain
In fathomless laughter
A sudden flight
Of white swans
In a cobalt sky
Sweetened tears
Drunk
From a bloodied mouth
This the life
Of one
Branded
By Thee

291

What need I for this robe of a warrior
When I long to be Thy lover?
Under the pink of thy silken blouse
Hide the undented steel of this armour
Wear inside thy flowing starry skirt
Heavy weather beaten boots of spike
And as you answer the call of the cuckoo
Or sigh with longing at the orange moon
Your ears will pick the whisper of a falling leaf
And when you melt in the arms of your paramour
Let not thy dagger fall to the ground
For it takes a warrior brave
To be my lover true

292

I wash
The terribly stained
Mind cloth
In the perennial waters
Of Thy Name
But the loathsome red
Guilt tattered
Shames river
To curl into a pond
Leaving the gurgling ocean
With Summer's
Unrequited debt

293

In the midst
Of ugliness
My soul
Affirms Her tryst
With Beauty

294

Thou the steady flame
Into whose bosom
My flickering one
Longs to merge

295

The One in me
Longed to be many
Ages passed
As I waited
Bare bosomed
Stilled breath
Unseeing eyes
Then a feather touch
A play of light
On dark leaves
A trickling warmth
From numbed toe
To quivering crown
Spilling me over
To All
My fluid Self
Embraced
Continents
Creations
The One in me
Submerged in All

Older than the stars
Younger than the dew
Is my love
For you

Achhan Sundaran
Amma Vijayalaxmi
Ravee
Raghuu
Minnie
Rajneesh
Adithya
Roshan
Angelina
Jagrutie

In Eternal Gratitude …